cejc
265

How to Write a Review

by Cecilia Minden
and Kate Roth

CHERRY LAKE PUBLISHING · ANN ARBOR, MICHIGAN

CHERRY LAKE
Publishing

Published in the United States of America by Cherry Lake Publishing
Ann Arbor, Michigan
www.cherrylakepublishing.com

Content Adviser: Jeannette Mancilla-Martinez, EdD, Assistant Professor of
Literacy, Language, and Culture, University of Illinois at Chicago

Photo Credits: Page 5, ©iStockphoto.com/gbh007; page 10,
©Konstantin32/Dreamstime.com; page 11, ©iStockphoto.com/
SilviaJansen; page 16, ©iStockphoto.com/bowdenimages; page 17,
©Monkey Business ImagesDreamstime.com; page 20, ©Noam Armonn/
Dreamstime.com.

Library of Congress Cataloging-in-Publication Data
Minden, Cecilia.
 How to write a review/by Cecilia Minden and Kate Roth.
 p. cm.
 Includes bibliographical references and index.
 ISBN 978-1-61080-310-6 (lib. bdg.)—ISBN 978-1-61080-315-1
(e-book)—ISBN 978-1-61080-320-5 (pbk.)
1. Reportage literature—Technique—Juvenile literature. 2. Nonfiction novel—
Technique—Juvenile literature. 3. Exposition (Rhetoric)—Juvenile literature.
4. Creative writing—Juvenile literature. I. Roth, Kate. II. Title.
 PN3377.5.R45M56 2011
 808'.042—dc23 2011030944

Cherry Lake Publishing would like to acknowledge the work
of The Partnership for 21st Century Skills. Please visit
www.21stcenturyskills.org for more information.

Printed in the United States of America
Corporate Graphics Inc.
January 2012
CLSP10

Table of Contents

CHAPTER ONE

What Do You Think?

How do you decide which products to buy?

Every day you make choices. How do you decide? Maybe you talk to your family and friends. You listen to their ideas.

Consumers buy **products**. **Reviews** are written by people who have tried out the product. Music, movies, books, and toys are a few of the things people review. Reviews give consumers the information they need to decide which products to buy.

Your opinion counts! You can help others by learning to write a good review.

Reviews can help you decide which books to read.

To get a copy of this activity, visit www.cherrylakepublishing.com/activities.

ACTIVITY

Choose the Product

In this activity you will choose a product that you will review.

HERE'S WHAT YOU'LL NEED:
- Pencil
- Paper

INSTRUCTIONS:
1. Make a list of products you use that you could review.
2. Include products you use often and really like or really dislike.
3. Choose one to review.

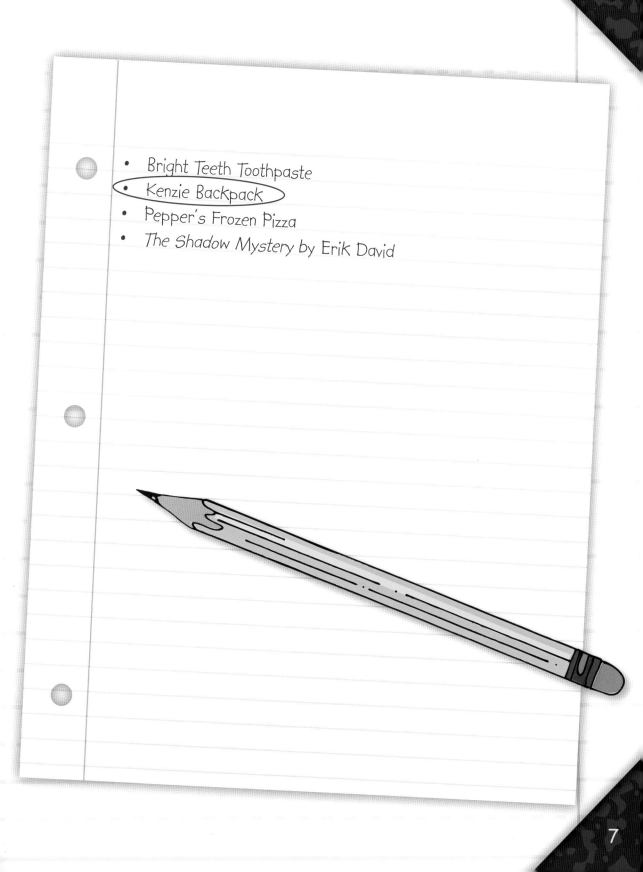

- Bright Teeth Toothpaste
- Kenzie Backpack
- Pepper's Frozen Pizza
- The Shadow Mystery by Erik David

CHAPTER TWO

What Is It?

When you review a product, you need to tell readers all about it. First you need to give a **description** of the product. What is its purpose? What does the product look like? What is the size and color? What is its shape? How does it look and feel? What else do you think a person reading your review might want to know?

Does the product come in different sizes or colors?

ACTIVITY

Describe the Product

In this activity you will write a few sentences to describe the product you are reviewing.

HERE'S WHAT YOU'LL NEED:
- Pencil
- Paper

INSTRUCTIONS:
1. Describe the purpose of the product. Why did you buy it? What will you use it for?
2. Describe what the product looks like.

To get a copy of this activity, visit www.cherrylakepublishing.com/activities.

I need a really good backpack for school that will last all year. I bought a Kenzie backpack. It is 14 inches high, 11 inches wide, and 6 inches deep. It comes in red, blue, and green. The backpack is made of heavy material and has padded shoulder straps. There are two side zippered pockets. It weighs less than a pound. It costs $17.99.

CHAPTER THREE

Does It Work?

Think carefully about all of the product's features.

Take time to **evaluate** the product you are reviewing. Try out all of the **features**. For example, if you are reviewing a backpack, decide if the zippers work well. You've tried out the product. Now decide if it works the way you think it should. Is there something about the product that doesn't work correctly? What would you change about the product? In your opinion, what is great about the product? Is it something you will keep using? Is the product worth the price you paid for it? Did you get what you paid for?

Take careful notes as you evaluate the product.

To get a copy of this activity, visit www.cherrylakepublishing.com/activities.

ACTIVITY

Evaluate the Product

In this activity you will add a paragraph to your review. It will explain your evaluation of the product.

HERE'S WHAT YOU'LL NEED:
- Pencil
- Paper

INSTRUCTIONS:
1. Write a paragraph to share your evaluation of the product.
2. Answer these questions:
   - What are the best and worst features of the product?
   - Does the product work the way you think it should?
   - Is there anything about the product you would change?
   - Is the price of the product a fair price?
3. Use details to support your ideas.

The Kenzie backpack is made of thick nylon fabric. It looks like it will last the whole school year. The padded shoulder straps are comfortable even when the pack is full. The zippered pockets on the side are handy. They keep small things from getting lost in the bottom of the bag. This bag is on the small side, however. It won't hold too many books and papers. The choice of colors is limited. The price seems fair.

CHAPTER FOUR

How Does It Compare?

Comparisons are a great way to tell people about products.

We can compare things we like to **similar** products. That way we can decide which one we like best. For example, you may like one brand of chocolate ice cream more than another. Reviews compare products that are similar. They explain how one product is better or worse than another and why. This can help give consumers a good understanding of the products. They can pick the one that has the features they like best.

Compare the Product

In this activity you will add a paragraph to compare the product to others that are similar.

HERE'S WHAT YOU'LL NEED:
- Pencil
- Paper

INSTRUCTIONS:
1. Write a paragraph to compare the product to other products.
2. Answer these questions:
   - Have you used a product that is similar?
   - How is the product you are reviewing better or worse than others you have used?
3. Use details to support your ideas.

To get a copy of this activity, visit www.cherrylakepublishing.com/activities.

Last year I had a Buster's backpack. It was bigger than the Kenzie. It came in a wider choice of colors. The price was a little less. The material for the Buster's bag was thin. It tore before the end of the school year. The Buster's bag only had one side pocket, and it snapped shut. The shoulder straps were padded, but the Kenzie straps have more padding and are more comfortable.

CHAPTER FIVE

Do You Like It?

Be honest about the product when you write your review.

End your review with your **recommendations**. This means you tell others whether or not they should buy the product. Try to be fair. Consider all of the good and bad points you discovered. If you didn't like the product, explain why you did not like it. If you liked the product, point out what makes it special.

A person reading your review might make a decision based on what you say. Ask yourself if you could make a decision based on your review.

People might decide what to buy based on your review.

To get a copy of this activity, visit www.cherrylakepublishing.com/activities.

ACTIVITY

Recommendations

In this activity you will write the last paragraph of your review. This is when you will make your recommendations.

HERE'S WHAT YOU'LL NEED:
- Pencil
- Paper

INSTRUCTIONS:

1. Write a paragraph to tell others if they should buy this product or not. Answer these questions:
   - Should someone buy this product? Why or why not?
   - What is the product good for?
   - Who will like the product?
2. Use details to support your ideas.

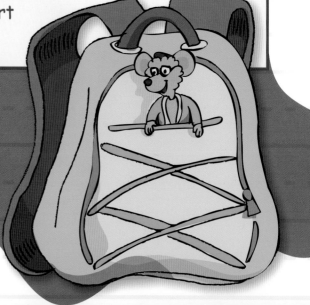

I would recommend a Kenzie bag but in a larger size. The price is a little higher, but it has more color choices. The heavy fabric, comfortable straps, and zipper pockets make this a great backpack. I won't have to worry about a ripped backpack this year!

CHAPTER SIX

Share Your Ideas

Now you can share your review with others. Maybe they will buy a product based on your review. What would you like to review next?

Ask your friends what they think of your review.

STOP!
DON'T WRITE
IN THE BOOK!

To get a copy of this activity, visit
www.cherrylakepublishing.com/activities.

ACTIVITY

Take a Final Look!

Ask yourself these questions as you reread your review:

☐ YES ☐ NO Did I choose a product that I know a lot about?

☐ YES ☐ NO Did I describe it with a lot of details?

☐ YES ☐ NO Did I evaluate the product fairly?

☐ YES ☐ NO Did I compare it to other products that do similar things?

☐ YES ☐ NO Did I make a final recommendation of whether someone should buy it or not?

☐ YES ☐ NO Did I use correct grammar and spelling?

Glossary

consumers (kuhn-SOO-murz) people who buy and use products

description (di-SKRIP-shuhn) words that create a picture in the mind of a person who reads or hears them

evaluate (i-VAL-yoo-ate) to decide the value of something

features (FEE-churz) particular parts or qualities of a person, place, or thing

opinion (uh-PIN-yuhn) a personal feeling or belief about someone or something

products (PRAH-duhkts) things that are made and sold

recommendations (rek-uh-men-DAY-shuhnz) suggestions that a person or product is good or worthwhile

reviews (ri-VYOOZ) pieces of writing that give the writer's opinions about books, movies, or products

similar (SIM-uh-lur) having many features in common

For More Information

BOOKS

Kamberg, Mary-Lane. *The I Love to Write Book: Ideas and Tips for Young Writers*. Milwaukee, WI: Crickhollow Books, 2008.

Olien, Rebecca. *Kids Write! Fantasy & Sci Fi, Mystery, Autobiography, Adventure, and More!* Nashville: Williamson Books, 2005.

WEB SITES

On-lion for Kids!—Reviews

kids.nypl.org/reviews/

Visit this New York Public Library site to read kids' reviews of books, movies, music, and Web sites.

Spaghetti Book Club—Book Reviews by Kids for Kids

www.spaghettibookclub.org

Check out this site to read book reviews and submit your own reviews.

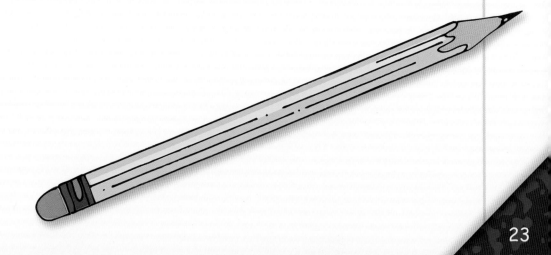

Index

About the Authors

Cecilia Minden, PhD, is the former director of the Language and Literacy Program at Harvard Graduate School of Education. She earned her doctorate from the University of Virginia. While at Harvard, Dr. Minden also taught several writing courses. Her research focuses on early literacy skills and developing phonics curriculums. She is now a full-time literacy consultant and the author of more than 100 books for children. Dr. Minden lives with her family in Chapel Hill, North Carolina. She likes to write early in the morning while the house is still quiet.

Kate Roth has a doctorate from Harvard University in language and literacy and a master's degree from Columbia University Teachers College in curriculum and teaching. Her work focuses on writing instruction in the primary grades. She has taught kindergarten, first grade, and Reading Recovery. She has also instructed hundreds of teachers from around the world in early literacy practices. She lives in Shanghai, China, with her husband and three children, ages 3, 7, and 10. Together they do a lot of writing to stay in touch with friends and family and to record their experiences.